TOMORROW'S
BRIGHT
WHITE
LIGHT
JAN
CONN

TOMORROW'S
BRIGHT
WHITE
LIGHT

JAN
CONN

Jan Conn (signature)

ENVS 3240
Creative Writing for Environmental
Scientists

TIGHTROPE BOOKS

March 2024

Tightrope Books
#207-2 College St
Toronto ON M5G 1K3
www.tightropebooks.com

Typesetting by Kris Westerlaken
Cover design by Deanna Janovski
Cover art by Annemarie Buchmann-Gerber and Jan Conn
Author photo by Carl Schlichting

We thank the Canada Council for the Arts and the Ontario
Arts Council for their support of our publishing program.

**Canada Council
for the Arts**   **Conseil des Arts
du Canada**

**ONTARIO ARTS COUNCIL
CONSEIL DES ARTS DE L'ONTARIO**
an Ontario government agency
un organisme du gouvernement de l'Ontario

PRINTED AND BOUND IN CANADA

Library and Archives Canada Cataloguing in Publication

Conn, Jan, 1952–, author
         Tomorrow's Bright White Light / Jan Conn.

Poems.

ISBN 978-1-988040-14-1 (paperback)

         I. Title.
PS8555.O543T64 2016   C811'.54   C2016-901292-1

for Carlo

for Annemarie Buchmann-Gerber
(1947-2015)

also by Jan Conn

Red Shoes in the Rain (1984)

The Fabulous Disguise of Ourselves (1986)

South of the Tudo Bem Café (1990)

What Dante Did with Loss (1994)

Beauties on Mad River (2000)

Jaguar Rain (2006)

Botero's Beautiful Horses (2009)

Edge Effects (2012)

Canadian poet **Jan Conn** was brought up in southeastern Quebec. She now lives in Great Barrington, Massachusetts and is a professor of Biomedical Sciences whose research is focused on the genetics and ecology of mosquitoes. She has published eight previous books of poetry, most recently *Botero's Beautiful Horses* and *Edge Effects*.

Contents

1   Battered Civilization

3   The House Is Sleeping but Its Windows Are Wide Awake

4   In the Year Two Thousand Eleven

5   Ourselves Lit Up

6   I Make Things Up as I Go Along

8   Touch Me Anywhere to Begin: A Biography of Eva Peron

10   Lost Marsupials (The Marvels of Santa Rosa)

12   A Torrent of Sparkling Can No Longer

14   Don't Interrupt the Cosmos

15   Self-Portrait at Summer's End

16   On the Left Bank of the Itaya

17   Family Portrait in an Unmarked Car

18   Ankles Dipped in a Rising Tide

20   A Night like This

21   A Life Unlived Any Other Way

22   A River Named Inambari

24   Roadside Attractions

25   Lac-Mégantic

26   Heisenberg's Uncertainty

27   Spotlights, Not Daylight

28   Frontier Mentality

29   Event Horizon (Mexico)

31   Landscape with Stand-In for Horse

32   When the Known World Is Flat

36   Loreto

38   Urbanity

39   Animals Are Us

40   Melodrama Is Foreign to My Nature

41   Light Strikes What It Can

42   The Brazilian Sugar Industry Rises from Its Knees

43   Dreamtime: Arizona

44   Riff on Massive Ocean Waves

46   Transience

48   To Franz Kafka from His Right Hemisphere

49   The Highway Unfolds in Front of You
       Whenever You Close Your Eyes

51   Pinheiros District

52   Notes

53   Acknowledgements

Battered Civilization

A sock particle was detected in the supercollider.
Can we make time out of bacteria?
Trade genomes for another year
of elephants? A parody
of my pernicious scheme unravels
but the scheme itself
is silk.

Which is more pervasive, night mist
or provincialism?

The hidden world of buzz-saws shakes me from sleep.
I was trying to hold my own.
I don't like canned salmon, except the crunchy bones.
Above the city walls float medieval pennants.
Listen to Neil Young, you'll get it.

Into deepening blackness
lit by a branch of forsythia
I stride forward, edges inflamed, and
inch sideways out of my body.

I am all pause, all
hesitation.
A foot on carpet, a foot
on cold stone floor.
Of my earlier existence all that remains is a grey felt hat.

I release my internal structure.
It rises to the top
and floats.

Did I mention my undocumented status?
My recharged emotional state?
The big green fractal or tree, bent
and streaming in the hurricane-force wind.

Our *corpora callosa* are shrunken
by the wanton application of neurotoxins.

Something trails behind
my narrow yellow shoulders,
rolls in with the motorcycle.
I unpack the bangbox first,
catalyzing the situation in the baggage room.
Strains
of old Beatles tunes, doves moaning in the gridlocked attic.
I've an earlier century in mind, a time
when cotton bags were varnished for carrying water.

The House Is Sleeping but Its Windows Are Wide Awake

The sensation of being late emanates from the stones set sideways
          in the wall.

At the count of three I lean into my bandana.

Welcome to the home of congestion and satori. Bring me your
          in-need-of-a-valve-job, your squealing wheel bearings.

If you're not from here, you won't believe that a bird lives
in every waterfall.

Or that since breakfast I've been scanned by a dozen remote sensors.

On the fourth day the music of chandeliers emanates from an
          en plein air ballroom.

I stumble from room to room expecting at every glance to see you—
strangers are washing the walls.

I'm only built to withstand shocks below a certain threshold.

Since nothing is equal to the task before me, I turn around—

In the Year Two Thousand Eleven

Scent of wild cherry kindling lingers in the patchwork
building, cast-iron stove still ticking over, warm to the
gloved touch. We have skidded to a halt, breathless, nervy,
guided here by a finger gliding across a small screen.

The dock has been jimmied from its pilings, quagmired on shore,
wood grain magnified beneath a slick of ice. Positioned to catch
roof run-off, a wooden barrel slips its hoops. We posit
a sculpture of dock, metal, and nearby rock, execution

iffy (acetylene torch, glue gun), but plausible.
Drawn to the edges of hemlock light,
we cantilever ourselves upward for the singular view
of the creature—upright, teetering

on a snow bank. Its arms are old propellers with crusty,
frostbitten tips. Metal birdcage for a head.
Below it are silvered fish houses, nominally
unremarkable, voltaic in this swarming light. One of us has traced

on the windcombed snow the blurred outline
of our former home. There is no explanation
for the seething promiscuity of white, or the bird skulls dangling
at the creature's side. On the edge

of the coast, the horizon is punctuated by twig-like
antennae. The green metallic hysteria
we thought of as extreme sky
is an ice cliff, looming, fresh from Antarctica.

Ourselves Lit Up

       Some learned from David Bowie
the brilliant idea of rotating one's own image.
Some got it wrong. I

       gulped so much homemade night
it was breakdown territory.

I considered removing to a smooth pale tub
and lapping cool lush tea
or setting up shop in a prosperous ghost town.

       Now that I've glimpsed the four large red fish
hanging from his handlebars
I mean to re-evaluate my impression
of his youth.

When I press my lips together like this
it's a naked bivalve.

       Does anyone believe I pushed
a wheelbarrow of unrepentant snakes up that hill?

Let's add to this poem a sliver of Elizabeth Bishop
's pale dirty light. Now cue
the centred look, the inward gaze.

I Make Things Up as I Go Along

I'm in love with the pinkness of pink,
I tell myself as the story floats by,
sans my little chapter.
Time has lost track of me.

To distract myself I wonder
where the mosquitoes go
(under the house or into the woods?)
after they've had their fill
of my iron-flavoured blood.

I can't explore both inside and out.
Red is to pink as blood is to water.
When not wandering lonely as a cloud
my mind follows its nose

and arrives after some years or perhaps days
at the smell of fresh mint.
Which isn't pink, but my uncle
kept a sprig in his breast pocket.

Pink, the feverish colour.
How hot depends. Sharply

the rains cut spring in two.
But it's still tropical forest dry.
Distressed green. Sugar cane, sugar cane.
No wonder my mind
leapfrogs. It's rambunctious here,
not soft. Pink, but hard
as granite.

Touch Me Anywhere to Begin: A Biography of Eva Peron

The present as wreckage, as pinball arcade.

Just when you imagined the torment was over.

The investigation proceeded along a fault line.

If you detect the slightest hint of grandeur, eradicate it immediately.

She was spotted in an estancia near a river.

Every day being videotaped by a tiny tribe of microbes.

If a person is infallible, she has to draw the line somewhere.

For carnival she dressed as the unknown.

A local parade of sequined donkeys passes through her.

Do you pledge in favour of control or glory?

Evita's power bar doesn't bequeath power.

The tear in the fabric was an exclamation mark of pure displeasure.

Petals mixed with ash in a field, a red dirt road
that winds among the grasslands.

You propose a museum of economic theories.

Once in a while you are on the side of petty.

Alone in the alley with the ghost of an idea of reform.

You'll be seen but not heard.

A bare-naked premise, a path that only appears behind you.

Hundreds of dolls tied to a chain-link fence.

Wire silhouettes of humans in lieu of humans.

They closed all the stadiums.

Your body as never previously recorded.

Please make sure your arms are still connected to your torso.

The vast Patagonian sky, the massif, a dog on the half-frozen river.

She continues living in her old apartments.

The mother of all Argentina hidden from herself.

Wilful ignorance may be her strongest product line.

Cold, drizzle, damp. The empty sheep farms wheezing,
abandoned even by mice.

Rampant forgery at every level; the workplace chokes, sputters,

carries on.

The number of skydivers quadruples.

If only you knew.

Parties, goalies, the sharp whiff of testosterone.

The peeling paint of her embodied gesture.

Divinity, obscenity, inequality.

Her body to be laid painstakingly on crushed silk while we wait.

There are rhinestones to button up, a hat to liberate from its hat box.

Lost Marsupials (The Marvels of Santa Rosa)

In the market they appear
as opossum-skin hats, tins of ear bones.

Beneath the gaze of Orion
we count our lucky stars: *uno, dos, tres, cuatro.*

The snorer next door cracks the sound barrier,
the bar swings into action, the TV

in the room opposite is cranked to the max.
To whom should we bow down in thanks

for stereo sound? During their nuptial flight,
male termites compulsively crawl upward

into clothes, onto face, into ears and eyes. Morning
is filtered through the lens of their discarded,

translucent wings. Where do you live, we questioned
a local woman. She pointed to a mango tree,

produced a jar of mouse opossum eyes. *Who is the ecstatic
in your immediate or extended family,* asked the religious form.

We ourselves had no one, but the neighbours
had Lucia, who one night choked to death

on her tongue. From a shopkeeper we purchase
cilantro and fresh oregano. He gestures

toward a shack whose current tenants
(hens, guinea pigs in a wooden box)

he plots to evict. He'll retire
among those profusely blossoming morning glories.

The bath-house is guarded by that gecko—
the eyespots of the enormous cloaked moth won't protect it.

A Torrent of Sparkling Can No Longer

Only now has hunger reached me.

After cataract surgery do you continue to detect those
spectral shapes?

How does it feel, no longer possessing a skeleton
and those tiny blue eggs. Hip deep in blackened greenery.

Oh lonesome. Don't force feed me rocket fuel.
Did you jam the machinery with the dead bolt?

Do not puncture. Do not burden yourself with a slingshot
when a power saw will do.

Are you rubble yet, part of the big scenery?

Phase I involves bandits emptying sacks of *Toxoplasma*.
The chaos metre likes it.

Sonoran desert for a nominal fee! Happy sunbathing.

Ah, the decorative. The merely. If we downsize humans.
If in the harbour. Downwind of. If you catch

my drift. A verticality tethers you. Don't you think?

In the shrubbery she consoles herself.

Who invents these scenes?

Deerhunting on the moon. You know you want to.

Suit up. Twist ties will remain in place.
Is the kill site on your mind?

The power grid cannot be managed, the northwest perimeter
held against us.

Don't Interrupt the Cosmos

I assemble two pint-size
cardboard dinosaurs, *T. rex*
and *Triceratops,* set them
on the hardwood floor.

Just when I feel relieved
to be doing my part
in diminishing interspecies strife
I hear ripping, aggressive noises.

Some people
have plastic hands and feet.

My dispirited neighbour
goes again to her porch door
to call her dead border collie, forgetting.

Time and electricity hum along.

I am tempted to put my head
inside the fridge
to visit the cooling eggs and milk.
They seem so peaceful.

I intended to say something
philosophical about modern thought
and the flow of time,
not like we are
their bleak centrepiece.

Self-Portrait at Summer's End

Finally packing to leave late in September,
never dreaming this would be the last time,
no dwelling on the screen door to the kitchen
with its eclipse of moths, their
extravagant plumose antennae, air-filled
fretwork, speckled with flicks of pigment,
radiant in the porch light's low wattage
star, susurration as the door sighs,
close out the impenetrable, stubborn blackness,
born of granite and gneiss.
Into this diorama,
from its fur-lined pocket under the eaves,
came the flying squirrel, patagium folded
and tucked, ghost-white hair to ghost-white
hair, a royal robe awaiting the signal
to unclasp—and by clotted-cream-yellow
daylight I tracked its flight from eastern
hemlock to mountain maple to white spruce, down,
down the hillside to the lakeside
where it stopped—at my feet
the crushed remains of an owl feast:
doll-saucer size top of the cranium, three long
whiskers, minute leather pouch of an ear capsule,
and I, in the smallest dory
from the neighbours, did not even
slow down, I, a tomboy, lithe and spare,
wild summer-girl-spirit, rowed and rowed,
I could not stop.

On the Left Bank of the Itaya

Ruinous, the heat along the Malecón, and the pathways
to the river through yucca and soccer fields remain

unknown to me. Here we elect politicians by marking an X
through a tree, a chick, a house, or a boat. After a week

the former mayor is released from jail, more charges
pending. He's running again, humidity is high, memory short.

Upriver, oil exploration mocks the concept
of arable land, bottled snowmelt from the Andes lacks last season's

cachet. The entrepreneurial spirit flags. At the city's exit
we're in a sea of hats—some orange brimmed, others

trying on the striped effect, the blues fall short on brightness
like the other brand in a laundry detergent ad. We wonder

what hit us. Then it hits us again. Lime green helicopter
on a deep green field. Beneath the hats, fishermen

down from high mountain streams stocked with fish
we'd love to have heard of, their copter grounded, something

mechanical. In the magical down-thrusting circle of the blades,
the local vegetation flattens and shines. Hard drinking ensues.

Last person standing wields the wrench.

Family Portrait in an Unmarked Car

The ace of clubs turns up at every party on the block
and in the parking lot where our neighbours dwell—

new lives in old cars. It gets dark early.
Our cars and our lives are uninsured, our rust-free chassis

are guaranteed to last and last. Shaving, then applying
lipstick in a rear-view mirror, is a lost art, he murmurs

to his son. In winter, we'll run low on fuel,
station ourselves in the basement of that shrink-wrapped

renovation. When security insists we move along,
we'll bark a lot. You'll be a great dog, says the father,

sliding out the door.

Ankles Dipped in a Rising Tide

Alerted by nickel-encrusted skeletons
or sea hunters' knives glued to bookshelves
on the VIA Rail Express,

we can be daughters and sons of old Canadian paperbacks—
or is it too late?

Pack me sheaths of sugar cane and a mass
of amaryllis, beneath which I might kneel,
borrowing a ritual for these cloud-tipped afternoons.

Prayers absent, I recite something moth-eaten,
a litany of rhapsodic elements
saved from the vanishing.

The perfect space for me: a jungle gym
in winter, hoar frosted, iced.

No one's sleep will be disturbed,
least of all that of Jacques Cartier.

I finally find the only open bodega in town,
but am too old to be served.

My short-term goal is to escape that guitarist—
her bodice of plastic percussion instruments
is stuck in a minor key.

•

Except by repeated non-seeking,
the path to the old orchard cannot be found.

I could admire the apples descending,
bouncing lightly on a cushion of vetch.

I could not cease screaming when my beloved
found another.

I could push through
a hundred windows—shattered behind me.

I could mimic peacocks shrieking on a shed roof
but not their plumage, those far-seeing eyes.

A Night like This

All the snow knives
disappear from northern towns.
Unexpected manifestations of grey
swarm from patches of fog.

Somewhere beyond our hearing
a dock, a boat, a string of lakes, portaged
under optimal conditions, food caches,
survival a matter of luck and good

timing. Stragglers of the diminished
herds, a few caribou pass us by,
vanish. Designer rocks in clusters, periscope-
shaped to record our every move.

A Life Unlived Any Other Way

In my suit of butterflies
      I am unprepared to confront army ants.

The ammo owners in this village are emperors.

Strolling alone to my tourist hotel
down the rain-smeared dirt road, followed
                  by a cloud,

I step—swiftly—into dappled shade.

At the edge of the edge   I pause.

The Renaissance did not reach
every corner of the globe.

Only thing holding up that scarred
                and grieving tree
is its supporting cast of lianas.

Under pressure, I am like myself
      only worse.

(I invite Goya
      to be my valentine.)

A River Named Inambari

Cast downriver
on long golden strings, the children of miners.

Presumed missing, locally extinct:
the giant river otter (chirr, chirr);
the charmless sting rays hidden in shifting sandbars,
little brown bats, decorous epaulettes, in a row
down the trunk of a palm tree.
We were tormented by flies all morning, then

in a 4 x 4, careened and jounced in and out of the river,
stained with gold and mercury.
On a tiny island of calm while the driver poles

for water depth, we watch wasps construct
something, probably useful, from saliva, chewed stems.
The few visible miners are so industrious,

dredging, sorting, plotting.
Not one bird. Even the katydids
tuned up elsewhere.

Twice we abandoned the vehicle,
crowded into small, swift boats, raced through
riffled, clay-coloured effluent, recoiling

from splashes. On a mud road a man tried to sell us
a gold-plated mermaid
undulating on the palm of his hand.

One last sprint in a boat, where in a ledger
the captain wrote our names,
and pressed us to wear life jackets.

Light receded on the farther reaches
of the river, curving to the west.
We were narcoleptic, knowing

what the dark could induce,
yet gripped, intoxicated, by deepening
mineral dusk. Our departure created space,

a design unfathomable as Nazca markings, subject
to radical interpretations, auguries.
Conversing with the parrot on her shoulder,

a young prostitute disappeared into the camp.
Reluctantly, the Andes relinquished their hold
on the night-licked Inambari.

Roadside Attractions

Seduced by the road, or drawn by subconscious ancestral
migratory routes, we enter the Ontario Greenbelt—

tall invasive reeds lay down their
highways of rhizomes, impossible to control or to learn

to love. Local municipalities instead purchase spring sale
leather couchettes. Really, is there a choice?

Cattails, where are you? Let it be recorded
that phlox is running riot, hitching rides to cottage country

in wooden boxes inside car trunks, in the beds of pick-ups,
a one-way ticket from garden centre to outcrop,

harridan pinks arm-in-arm with formal whites,
defying local hybrid bans. Somewhere between

the Living Waters Assembly of God and Rivers of Life
Fellowship Centre, we become gloriously, hysterically

lost, having stopped for just a moment
to pour our souls into summer.

Lac-Mégantic

Rounding the curves in an era super charged and pugnacious,
its stock alternately breaking out or breaking
bad, this CPC-1232 tank car is
backlogged. On the outside,
sleek, submarine-like, subversive,
the inside pervaded by a greed-filled
Carboniferous consciousness—
the scent of bitumen dislocates the air.
And we are overjoyed having discovered that the light from
trilliums originates in the Triangulum
Galaxy, and the luscious pink of spring beauties
in the Valley of Dolls.
Human community as we know it
already unrecoverable
such that we look back upon Genghis Khan
with unalloyed nostalgia.
And here, no sign of sky,
just fiercely raging fires circled in red
and noxious smoke
on the geologist's map: Lac-Mégantic, Gogama
twice, Plaster Rock, Edmonton.

Heisenberg's Uncertainty

Voodoo queen, toes immersed in swamp water,
an after-image of swept-away buildings.
Everything below the flood line is up for grabs.
At the heart of each sigh, Fats
Domino inserts our inability to place one foot
in front of the other.
Here's the Mississippi, lips
curled, lapping at the base of the Crescent City
Connection. Stand back from the yellow line,
away from the floor-to-ceiling,
tell-tale wobble in the glass.
She points, from the 34th floor,
Can you see the Gulf?
Inside her voice there are breakers,
swells slosh up and down the corridors—
sleep is elusive. That sojourn in Topeka—
X-ray of room, dog, self. Failed ads on Craigslist,
advice on artwork compressing her chest.
Midday and midnight blue increasingly
indistinguishable. Up close,
her lips quiver.
The only place she ventures
that isn't a full-bore failure of nerve,
wit, or simply bad genes, is the Quaker meeting hall
basement. *I want the stillness
of no more wanting,* I think she said.

Spotlights, Not Daylight

He's backed up against
an extraordinary block of black.
The situation—bright flesh tint—
calls for boldness, but he is
stock still, songs
logjammed in his throat.
The family room fills up
with the tang of fruit flies.
Rows and rows of light bulbs
on the ceiling like at a casino.
The sockets are zapped.
His friends are not at home, but
pressing themselves unwillingly
facedown on the shimmering asphalt,
cocaine in a pocket.
Now he is naked inside a deep
charcoal grey, magnetic weight
on his chest. It's late in the afternoon.
With his throat he makes a sound.
Out in the yard he and his friends
used to take turns dying, extra points for
the most disgusting ketchup substitute.
A door opens. An hour passes.
He thinks about scrambling
up onto the roof where the laundry
snaps and flutters, freeing the shirts,
then his friends from cocaine
and danger. He sees them
running through the streets,
just like that.

Frontier Mentality

More and more we turn to urban life where the next big thing
is being created as we speak, in which we might partake
as one member of a large community of those at loose ends

or disaffected. Single mothers disrupted by endless sleep-
deprivation. What possessed us to purchase a condo whose
single distinguishing attribute is a view of a reflection

of the Statue of Liberty? There must be some perks to living
in the shadow of that massive municipal electrical station—
like never having to recharge our iPhones. The weather here

is so mild that -40 in Nunavut is inconceivable. We buy full-
spectrum lights and dispense advice to our northern friends
about combating SAD by the daily application thereof.

If we're ashamed of the lack of pretension of our younger selves,
we don't let on. We've never been that fond of wine-tastings
with their over-the-top descriptions of nose, but we're trying to fit in.

Undue loyalty to a dream of home ownership,
college loans unforgiven, we're looking for the scam
that makes the ends crawl a little closer together.

Event Horizon (Mexico)

After many sips of mezcal our lips need a rest.

We can only gaze at each other in mirrors.

It's an exhausting holiday—Empress Carlota sailing to Paris
locked in her stateroom.

Taking our hand-woven jackets we return to the party.

The fortress at Yagul for the best views, the scandalous art bar
for nightlife.

Each of us recalls the narrative as a series of thresholds.

Now we're living on hands and knees.

●

In crisis mode you identify with a dog.

Around the central plaza are many horse-drawn carts but none
going to your destination.

Rumours persist you've sailed to the Mediterranean—
photos uploaded to a blog then taken down, postcards
(how quaint) from Seville with no return address.

I stand in the desert near the ruins surveying a landscape
rich with your imprint,
bougainvillea climbing like a rash.

In the roofless restaurant, masks above the bar
portray in tongues your erotic, nomadic life—
unpleasant to listen to during a meal, someone says on the way out.

We disappear for weeks then meet in a casual frenzy,
first-name-basis only. You
always find me, fresh from some breathless encounter.

Landscape with Stand-In for Horse

First thing he'd save in case of flood, a recently
acquired wooden horse

he was inspired to stripe, one-upping
his riverside competitors. They've smaller horses,

nothing so quixotic. Right now, he needs cash,
owes someone big. Spits on the bridle for luck,

smiles and smiles at the local kids, cell phones in hands,
indulged by grandparents, but they all move on

to a spiffed-up river steamship circa 1906 adorned
with hand-stitched Portuguese lace—yes, this vessel

formerly plied the lawless Putumayo. Even with the offer
of discounted sombreros, it's a sluggish day, tourists

sparse. Soon he can't resist and mounts—
it's not as if he were born to it. He yanks the reins,

creating multiple blurry selfies, conjuring false trails
on Facebook. He's heard the stories.

When the Known World Is Flat

Earth you know is round but
                    seems flat.

You can't trust
your senses.

                    —Frank Bidart

Provisional Exit Strategy

Speaking of his Metabolism buildings, the architect
insists they slowly mutate, pure green,
but how to distinguish this from corrosion?
When the planktonic shift rocks the coastline
we're in runaway mode,
the auto mechanic travels by train,
a frame-by-frame evolution
of a gasoline pump from a man's torso and arm.
At all times, follow the cowboy code.
The skulls at auction are not human.

Antidote for a Dream

Stealing milk I glimpse my photo. Believe me,
I had a non-neglected childhood
fuelled by skating rink feuds.
Poster child for that striking state,
"disturbed." I'm not missing, just
aloft, balloon basket crammed with every
incriminating milk carton in town. I
pitch them overboard in gangs. When I touch down at
Chalk River, children mob me,
clamouring for autographs on shreds of silk.

The Effacement of Memory

We shimmy up telephone poles for the long view:
the east coast uprooted and ravaged.
That savage grinding and crushing
of concrete barriers, dunes effortlessly
razed. Afraid to be alone with so many
grains of sand, GPS on the rocks, we head
inland, past a woman face down
in her swimming pool, a flower nodding
on her hat. The small reserve of sunscreen
we salvaged has leaked away.

Small Cut Surfaces

Even in this storm the back door is held open
by a slender white-washed string. Did he
misunderstand the rules? He dove headfirst
into the hurricane—
Piercing the passing blue: tangled remnants
of witch hazel and hickory, the plainspoken
brown of a moose. This stream flows north
to the St. Lawrence near where he was born.
To the rescue worker he whispers, I'm here
but my jacket is travelling first class.

Bimodal Emotional Syndrome

I fashion a second self: a fusion of declamation
and deviant DNA profile.
The balm of late-night violet
versus the jangle
of paternal orange, section by section.
I'm all for improvising stains and stabs (on paper)
at the local, or chanting in unison
to egg on an avalanche of branches
from the top of that unlikely looking tree.

A darker, more emblematic performance art.

We Require Calibration

on Centigradestreet, our blood lacking
some essential ion
or mineral salt. Driving to Red Deer and back,
the time of our lives: bald-headed
November, cornstalks smashed, invasive weeds
skeletal in ditches.
Troubled and taciturn, days erupt.
Our father's teeth, after sixteen years
of chemo. Seeking solace someplace,
aren't we?

State of Being

My hometown has been plundered
for rare earth metals. In this sheer pink slip
I protest. Acres of blighted boysenberries—
my rural aspect. Birds that appear drab
may be spellbinding in ultraviolet light.
The chemists, the data-miners, the landscape
geneticists, the brown bear named Lemon Drop:
these are the survivors. Think of me
alone in my woods with a chain saw
and a 5-kilo sledge.

Loreto

This is water's world
And the works of men are vanishing
                    —Alice Oswald

After a morning downpour all is as well
as can be, it's Iquitos, roads and buildings
squat on near-white sand, a perennial floodplain
whose only allegiance is to the great rivers
and then the sea, far to the east.
But nobody dwells on this today.
Stung by circumstance, bad job options
or none at all. The Fitzcarraldo Bar
fails spectacularly in its efforts
to recreate the previous century's boomtown mood,
and in the flashpoint of the present
one is brought up short. Across the water,
a scant kilometre from where you stand, a few scarred
rubber trees sway collectively in heat haze.

In a persistent slouch against doorframe,
shirtless and barrel-chested, like as not
with toothpick, middle-aged, lightly held
in the vaunted bosom of family, you're one
in this remote region of fortune hunters,
timber extractors, ex-militia, daily joy-riding your
recalled Silverado south along the shortest piece
of underfunded roadway
in the country. Past collapsing fish farms,
poorly executed agricultural

projects, rope failing to cinch loads of plantain,
morning-glory-draped foundations of the latest resort
of some disastrous investment firm, shell games
from the start. Still children queue up to feed

orphaned manatees, and a flashy
kingfisher alights, bearing twice
its daily allotment of fish.
All the way to Nauta, gunning it past any moving
form of conveyance, you need more asphalt
under your belt. You are not the person crouched
over burning logs creating endless briquettes,
nor the day-labourer,
security guard, or even the poacher who avidly
searches for wild palms
to slash from them their hearts. The inhabitants
regard your daily arrivals with something
akin to pity, your truck decelerating
at the river bank at unrecorded speeds.

Urbanity

Just so's you know, we're still in the
game. Treefall, Glenfiddich, creamed spinach
on melba toast. Amazing how these clouds
puff up like tempestuous Elizabeth's royal sleeves
then fizzle, comes no rain.

We slouch past the in-another-lifetime five-and-dime,
ghosts of disintegrating shoplifted items
flutter on a taut clothesline.
Stevie Ray Vaughan's the one I want back,
rocking blues guitar, brocade

shirt. Local colour, even Texan, wasn't enough.
We prefer our news feed
online, no back story, no
human interest. Check that tree species
off the list—a pale green wash. The guy's pet ferret

sharpening its teeth on a security fence.
Sinister, rooster-headed men in tuxes arrive.
Someone who shouldn't be
is monkeying with the numbers.

Animals Are Us

There's a way the afflicted can suck all the oxygen
from an enclosed space, aware
they're more likely to be hunted down.

How superior we feel when we provide for them,
the three-legged Chihuahua, a temporary home, the
crocodile reared in the sewer a free pass to the zoo.

•

To engage with the wasps
that seek a slight imperfection in the wooden deck
to build a home, and fear them on behalf
of my sweetheart, severely allergic, is to run counter
to a lifetime of entomological indulgence—

•

Well, something has given me this body, and the octopus
his. Scantily clad he streams from side to side
of the Mariana Trench, eclipsing the chasm
between body and mind. *How early I learned the body
as landscape too dangerous for direct approach.*

Melodrama Is Foreign to My Nature

The present me and the past me
will not align. Still in search
of Elmer's Glue, just like at age nine,
I await transit to a new condition, charting
binge possibilities. Collage
is so in: glue, scissors, each still life preening,
elbowing others aside. I'm in training
to represent the Rauschenberg Gap
between art and life.
Who admits to liking vinyl siding?
I salvage bunny ears
from the cast-off grainy print of a TV set.
I won't stand in this iridescent
column. By error I rent the shadow
of an apartment building, celebrating
all the ledges I have never dusted.
That me viewed through stained glass
is not subhuman, only miserable.
I'm forced to abandon summer:
the boarded-up lighthouse
blocked my paths to sunlight
one by one.

Light Strikes What It Can

Those who inherit the loneliness of the North Pole
must speak or break.
Clairvoyance dwindles as the days shorten. Outlines
blur. The kid warms his hands in an ice bucket,
feet in a dream of the Arctic Ocean.
Across sundered tundra, he drives an iceberg
into a black so dense it sparks
and stutters.
Plains undulate north, indecipherable
in tarnished medium grey, horizon-grey,
their beauty weightless but registering in his mind.
Below a certain temperature
sounds amplify, shift spectra, alter childhood hearing
so he doesn't react—much—
to the faint-faint crunch of crackled ice.
The bears, the same scruffy white as the snow.

The Brazilian Sugar Industry Rises from Its Knees

The ingenious solution to your factory space crisis?
That was her. Rapid
assembly of the crystallizer, levered
through the roof into the space
it couldn't fit.
A popular species of sugarcane
harvester she rejects, seeing its potential
for rapid breakdown,
corrosion in the crushing process. The back-up
crystallizer, displayed
on a flatbed swinging by, proudly
reigns over the universe of floating techno-
functional machinery and farm hands. Migration
on the rise. No wonder.

Exhausted but performing solo her vital task,
the mechanistic and logical holding their own
against a long history of self-doubt and obsession,
she wonders what would happen
in her plane of existence
should she enter the incorrect code for the formula
she comprehends
beyond the meaningful decimal.

Conversing with the plant manager
over some detail of product planning,
she understands him to say
every hillside is available
for the pleasure of our billboards.

Dreamtime: Arizona

I want to be transported to the Sonoran desert
in time to sip a salt-rimmed glass of sunset,
watch *palo verde* mysteriously transform
from memory's green to midnight sheen.
Nondescript crosses planted in family groups
pepper the flatlands
and the orange-crush bandanas of ocotillo
wave before roving patrols of self-appointed
homeland warriors: over here, over there, and, oh, Arizona,
I paddle in the diminishing aquifers
of your burgeoning cities, in this all-but-perfect state
for retirees, asthmatics,
and builders of underground bunkers
who got the market down cold.
In the hot winds, eucalyptus combusts spontaneously,
creosote bushes crackle and snap, the sky so lit up
that travellers marvel at whatever is being celebrated,
even unto the speed limitless
highways, where I intend to race the reintroduced
Mexican grey wolf to the finish line, take
my winnings to the nearest casino and kickstart
the blackjack table, wave my giant blue diamond ring
at the admiring crowd.

Riff on Massive Ocean Waves

the subtle pressure of wonder
leaking away

                               into ornamentation, pure
                               and simple

terror an essential partner—
let's heighten the beautiful
to the sublime, be knocked
off our feet, tsunamied
senseless

                               who can argue with
                               translucent inundation

surfer girl with a little curl
Hokusai-in-your-face, towering
beaten eggwhite wunderkind

                               surf's washed up, sandblasted

we paddle our outrigger
up and over renegade waves

                               on vacation, rippling south

send me just one rogue Tahitian breaker,
an element of surprise

                               awakened by duckcall,
                               snow falling, startling white
                               on Pang Gulang

pass the ink and watergun

don the coral snake wetsuit,
shimmy up the nearest tree

Transience

Midsummer, where I spent a few days,
has been rerouted so it's more difficult
to locate. You always said it was the best
season, fragrance of thyme after lightning,
before the humidity set everyone's
teeth on edge, murder rates climbing.
We followed Andy Goldsworthy's

stone installation as far as we could
then I took your hand.
Our take on his ephemeral
art might be a good luck charm, or maybe personal drama
on a fine scale. Such ventures tend

not to end well. We both balked
before the summers of my youth. In the dimly lit
hallways of the geology museum,
rebellious and sulky, I was forced
to repeat the quartz mantra *one silicon*

to two oxygen, each oxygen shared between two
tetrahedra. Here along a glacial moraine
I did mandatory interval training, but the trail
runs out at the painted backdrop of the Rockies.
Perhaps shifting those sedimentary layers

was as close to June and to you as I could
ever get. Too much truth laid bare.
Alongside the stone spiral, ants
were foraging everywhere. I hadn't noticed
until I crouched down.
Some of them were carrying
pieces of Andy Goldsworthy underground.

To Franz Kafka from His Right Hemisphere

From platinum-rimmed thimbles we drank brut.
This was love the size of a postage stamp.

Oh the ants we crushed, the murdered roaches...
In the end, desire may be no different from any other story.

Please spray the peonies a little, swap
one emotional valence for another.

Exciting kind of stillness, neither destroying nor
delivering a long letter to your father.

Some faint awareness of you, in a quiet street,
a few drops of rain from the linden tree.

It's been a long time since we chanted the word Byzantine
out loud. In Munich

we lodge with a piano that won't tolerate off-Broadway,
pedal-warmers, key toner.

We share a belief in dissonant information. Why
make breakfast? Why not just revise your diary?

The Highway Unfolds in Front of You Whenever You Close Your Eyes

I run toward the unravelling Dewey Decimal System.

Inside parentheses I am surrounded by the irationality
of pointed objects.

For days I shiver, for days I am scentless.

Nowhere is the salt-seeking balm of the sea, the pollen
returned to its pistil, the grass given back its green.

I want to be both noun and verb.

Clustered with my sweethearts around an oasis of time in the violet heat
of late afternoon.

Crouched beside the silence of a glacier.

We become indistinguishable from the rapid, downward slide.

Air hisses one-way through the wing veins: costa, subcosta, radius,
media, as energy, as cloud.

Through a tiny house, green-shuttered.

Suppose I remove all trace of the weapon except for a brushstroke
of gun-metal grey—

Enigma, ambiguity, loss.

The continual present is all that is allowed.

Pinheiros District

Most appear positively occupied, chatting or smoking
in the privatized public space,
tethered to electronic devices, orange uniforms
surpass the new matte black anticipating
sprayed and splashed graffiti.
We run out of expletives and energy, our anger
like the fires of Roraima that refuse to be contained.
She gets out here, in the neighbourhood of guitar stores,
dub and samba pick-up bands, a lack of eco-friendly
plantings. Enterprises flourish and disappear
the same week. Loyal customers,
you're a thing of the past. Parking lots proliferate,
spawned in some urban planner's pop-up factory
of sugar-charged cars. Though the residences they replace
are hard to recall in the ongoing pseudo-
gentrification that borrows as its banner
expedience, accessibility. At the corner, she's suddenly aware
everyone is side-stepping an offering to an Orixa
that has bloomed mid-sidewalk as dusk falls.
Amid the traffic cones, she hesitates, considering
the options. Either way, she'll be late.

Notes:

"I Make Things Up as I Go Along" is for Maria Anice Sallum.

"Lost Marsupial (The Marvels of Santa Rosa)" is for Marta Moreno.

"Transience" is in memory of Robert Tyhurst (1951-2014).

"To Franz Kafka from His Right Hemisphere" adapts fragments from the article "What Kind of Funny Is He?" by Rivka Galchen, *London Review of Books,* Vol. 36, No. 23, 4 December, 2014.

"Pinheiros District"—An Orixa is a spirit god of the Afro-Brazilian religion Candomblé.

Acknowledgements:

Early drafts of several poems were first published as noted below, some with different titles. I am very grateful for the support of all the editors of these literary magazines and journals, in print and online.

The Antigonish Review: "A River Named Inambari"

Arc: "Don't Interrupt the Cosmos,"
"In the Year Two Thousand Eleven"

The Best Canadian Poetry Anthology in English, ed. Sonnet L'Abbe, Tightrope Books, 2014: "Battered Civilization"

Canadian Poetries (http://www.canadianpoetries.com/): "A Life Unlived Any Other Way"

Contemporary Verse 2: "Family Portrait in an Unmarked Car", "Urbanity"

The Fiddlehead: "Ankles Dipped in a Rising Tide," "Melodrama is Foreign to my Nature," "Lost Marsupial (The Marvels of Santa Rosa)," "Heisenberg's Uncertainty," "Frontier Mentality," "To Franz Kafka from His Right Hemisphere"

Imaginarium 3: The Best Canadian Speculative Writing, ed. Sandra Kasturi and Helen Marshall, Chizine Publications, Toronto, 2014: "In the Year Two Thousand Eleven"

The Malahat Review: "Battered Civilization," "Transience," Self-Portrait at Summer's End"

Poems from Planet Earth, ed. Yvonne Blomer and Cynthia Woodman Kerkham, Leaf Press, 2012: "Riff on Massive Ocean Waves"

PRISM international: "Ourselves Lit Up"

Truck (www.halvard-johnson.blogspot.com.br/), October, 2015: "Spotlights, Not Daylight," "Light Strikes What it Can"

To Carl Schlichting, Diane Conn, Mary di Michele, Jane Munro, Susan Gillis, Stan Dragland, William Hunt, Julie Hedrick, Suzanne Hicks, Annemarie Buchmann-Gerber, Bessy Reyna, Jessica Treat and Martine Vermeulen, who contributed informed, intuitive readings and conversations, friendship and focus.

Composer Max Vinetz created a musical score for three poems: "Provisional Exit Strategy," "Antidote for a Dream," and "The Effacement of Memory." His composition was performed by Jennifer Beattie, *mezzo-soprano*, and Adam Marks, piano, at Art Song IV! Yale College New Music, at St. Anthony's Hall at Yale University, New Haven, CT, on Sunday, February 21, 2016. A marvellous gift, especially in February. I am deeply grateful to Max Vinetz for this collaboration, and to Joe Vinetz, for the introduction to Max.

I'm delighted to thank the fine and generous people at Tightrope Books: Jim Nason, first and foremost; Heather Wood for graciously and quickly handling the many details of organization, readings, all queries; and Deanna Janovski for her skilful copyediting.